EXPLORING HISTORY
Britain at War 1939~45

IAN GILMOUR

Oliver & Boyd

Contents

Map	Inside front cover
Introduction	3
1. The Beginning	4
2. Preparing for War	6
3. Crisis	10
4. If the Invader Comes	14
5. The Blitz	18
6. Shelters	22
7. At Home in Wartime	25
8. At Work	30
9. At Play	32
10. Victory	35
11. Finding Out About the War	38
Bibliography	39
Index	40
Time Line	Inside back cover

Topics for Workguides

1. The Coming of War
2. Dunkirk
3. If the Invader Comes
4. A Night During the Blitz
5. Air Raid Precautions
6. At Home in Wartime
7. At Work in Wartime
8. At Play
9. Victory and After
10. Thinking About the Evidence

Acknowledgements

The author and publishers would like to thank the following for permission to use copyright photographs:

BBC Hulton Picture Library cover, 4, 6, 15, 27 (top), 29, 33, 36, 37, 38; *Evening Standard* and the Low Trustees 14; D Fitzgerald (courtesy Devon County Library) 5 (right); Herts County Council Library Service 7 (left); Illustrated London News Picture Library 11, 12 (bottom), 17; Imperial War Museum 3, 9, 12 (top), 13, 14, 18, 19, 25, 27 (bottom), 31, 35; London Transport 23, 24, 30; City of Manchester Public Libraries 5 (left); *Punch* 24 (bottom); S & G Press Agency 7 (right), 8; John Topham Picture Library 21.

Illustrated by John Marshall

Oliver & Boyd
Robert Stevenson House
1-3 Baxter's Place
Leith Walk
Edinburgh EH1 3BB

A Division of Longman Group Ltd

This edition
© Oliver & Boyd 1982

ISBN 0 05 003347 6

Printed in Hong Kong
by Wah Cheong Printing Press Ltd.

Introduction

The Raid

It is November, 1940. The time is 5.30 pm, and you are having your tea. Suddenly you hear a loud wailing noise, rising and falling.

You dread this noise, but have come to know it well. It is the warning note of an air-raid siren. You know that you must take cover. Bombers are on their way. You leave your tea, collect your gas mask and, with your family, make your way into the garden. Here you have a small shelter, made of steel and covered with soil. This is your air-raid shelter. Though it is cold, dark and damp, you are lucky. Others have to shelter under their stairs. Some have to make their way to large public shelters.

Soon you hear the noise of aeroplanes, followed by the thud of exploding bombs. Again and again come the sharper bangs of the anti-aircraft guns. You are expert at telling how far away these noises are.

The raid seems to go on for hours, until you eventually fall asleep. Much later, your mother wakes you. The siren has given the all-clear signal, so you can go back to the house for breakfast. You have been lucky, because your house has escaped damage. You may not be so lucky tomorrow if the bombers return.

In 1940 and 1941 many British families shared this experience. It was the time of the 'blitz', when German bombers attacked towns in Britain.

A London street after an air-raid

Scenes like that above were common. It would bring back memories to many older people, who may be able to tell you about the blitz and other things that happened to them during the Second World War. Some of them might have been in the forces and involved in exciting events abroad.

Most people were not in the forces, or abroad. They were at home, but not out of the war. The Second World War involved everyone in Britain in some way, from the youngest to the oldest in the land. This book is about these people. It tells of dangers and hardships they faced - like the blitz. It is also about more ordinary things, and about the funnier side of the war which made it all more bearable. Here you will learn something of what it was like to live in Britain at war.

3

1. The Beginning

> Come on Auntie, let's go and make a cup of tea.

Stand By for an Important Announcement

On a sunny Sunday morning, the Prime Minister broadcast over the wireless:

I am speaking to you from the Cabinet Room at 10 Downing Street. This morning the British Ambassador in Berlin handed the German Government a final note, stating that unless we heard from them by 11 o'clock that they were prepared at once to withdraw their troops from Poland, a state of war would exist between us. I have to tell you that no such undertaking has been received and that consequently this country is at war with Germany.

Millions listened to that radio broadcast. It was Sunday, 3 September 1939. For days war had seemed likely. Look at the Time Line inside the back cover. You will be able to work out why people had been expecting war. Perhaps you can see why some had been expecting it for months. Now that war had come, there was a sense of relief. The uncertainty was over. There was a burst of activity to prepare for the days ahead.

1. *Which is the most important phrase in the Prime Minister's announcement?*
2. *Explain in your own words why Britain had gone to war.*
3. *If you had listened to this broadcast, what do you think your feelings would have been?*
4. *Find out how people you know learned of the outbreak of war, and how they felt.*

When the First World War began in 1914, the streets were filled with cheering crowds. The picture on this page shows a crowd in Downing Street in 1939.

1. *Which of these words would you choose to describe the mood of the people?*
   Excited   Sad   Happy   Silent   Anxious
2. *Suggest a reason why people should have felt this way in 1939.*

Preparing for the Worst

In 1939 everyone knew that war was a terrible thing. They expected there would be heavy air-raids on London, with German bombers dropping bombs and poison gas. Over 600 000 people might be killed in the first three months. Millions of cardboard coffins had been prepared.

1. *Study the Time Line at the back. Why were bomb and gas attacks on London expected?*
2. *What precautions might be taken to protect people from these dangers?*

The diary of a London woman tells of preparations that had been made. Here is part of her entry for September 3rd - the day war broke out:

The eye has become accustomed to sandbags everywhere, and to the barrage balloons, which spread over the sky like a silvery rash. Posting a letter is more interesting now, since the red pillar boxes have been done up in squares of yellow detector paint, which changes colour if there is poison gas in the air. Gas masks have suddenly become part of everyday equipment, and everybody is carrying the square cardboard cartons. Last night London was completely blacked out. The evacuation of London, which is to be spaced over three days, began yesterday.

Mollie Panter-Downes

1. Find and describe:
   (a) two precautions against poison gas;
   (b) two attempts to make bombing more difficult;
   (c) two precautions against the effects of bombs.
2. Which two preparations for war would most affect everyday life?
3. In one sentence, say what kind of warfare was feared most in 1939.

Left A crew tend a barrage balloon (people called them 'blimps') in a Manchester Park. Note the size of the balloon and the tethering wires. The balloons were to prevent bombers from flying low over targets.

Right Gas mask drill at school. Masks had to be checked to see that they fitted tightly.

2. Preparing for War

'Wear Something Light at Night' was the advice during the blackout!

Get That Light Out

The blackout began on 1 September 1939. It lasted in some form until May 1945. Blackout rules made it an offence to show a light during the hours of darkness. Houses, shops, offices, factories, street lights, cars, buses and trains were all affected. It was hoped that blackout would make it more difficult for enemy bombers.

1. *Explain in your own words what the blackout was.*

2. *How would it make things more difficult for bombers?*
3. *How would you blackout your house?*
4. *What dangers might blackout bring out of doors?*

Blackout was greatly disliked. It was a nuisance for everyone. At home shutters or blackout material had to be placed in position each night, and checked to see that no light escaped. One house in Cambridgeshire had 53 windows, which took 20 minutes to blackout each night.

Outdoors blackout brought danger. Vehicles were only allowed to show a small amount of light from their headlights. During the first four months of the war deaths due to road accidents were twice the normal figure. Posters warned people to be careful.

1. *Explain the picture on the left in your own words.*

Like most other aspects of wartime life, blackout had an amusing side too. One woman was seen trying to find her way by the light of glow worms placed on a mirror. Another was found in tears, unable to find her own house which she knew was somewhere nearby. A group of people came out of a village hall, and walked straight into the village pond. No wonder people were glad when it was all over, and the lights could come on again.

1. *What people do you think would: (a) find their jobs made more difficult by the blackout;*

(b) enjoy the blackout?

2. *Try to find out at home about the blackout, and about the difficulties and amusing things that happened.*

Gas

For the first few days of the war nearly everyone carried their gas masks. Soon, however, only a few people were to be seen with the square cardboard boxes. Masks began to appear on the shelves of lost-property offices.

In the end it did not matter. No gas was dropped on Britain during the war, but at least the country had been prepared. Apart from the millions of ordinary masks, special designs were made for babies and young children. You can see an example in the picture below.

1. *Government posters advised people always to carry their gas masks. Why do you think many people soon began to ignore that advice?*
2. *Altogether millions of pounds were spent on gas precautions. Gas was never used. Was the expense justified? Why?*

Evacuation

The children in the picture are being evacuated.

1. *Where do you think they would be going from? Where to?*
2. *Look for suitcases, bundles of possessions, gas mask containers, labels bearing children's names. Would you say the children are going for a long or a short stay?*

'Why are some mummies crying?'
'Because they can't come on holiday with us too.'

Schoolchildren, infants with their mothers, and expectant mothers were evacuated from large towns which might be bombed. They were to go to safer 'reception areas' in the country. They would be billeted on families living there. Between September lst and 3rd 1½ million people were evacuated. The table on the right shows towns from which evacuation was organised. Many others, mostly those who were better off, made their own private arrangements.

Towns which were evacuated		
Birkenhead	Hull	Salford
Birmingham	Leeds	Sheffield
Bootle	Liverpool	Smethwick
Bradford	London	South Shields
Clydebank	Manchester	Southampton
Coventry	Middlesbrough	Sunderland
Derby	Newcastle	Tynemouth
Dundee	Nottingham	Wallasey
Edinburgh	Portsmouth	Walsall
Gateshead	Rosyth	West Bromwich
Glasgow	Rotherham	West Hartlepool
Grimsby		

'They're pigs.'
'No they're not, they're sheep.'

Town Meets Country

Some children were astonished by the countryside and their new homes. Remember that most of the evacuees came from the poorer parts of our cities. In those days many had never been in the country before. Many were not used to baths or indoor toilets. Here an evacuee describes his new 'home':

Everything was so clean in the room. We were given flannels and toothbrushes. We'd never cleaned our teeth up till then. And hot water came from the tap. And there was a lavatory upstairs. And carpets. And something called an eiderdown. And clean sheets. This was all very odd.

Bernard Kops *The World's a Wedding*

The evacuees were not the only ones to be surprised:

Frantic householders asked what we were going to do about ridding them of the lice and filth which had invaded their homes. They had to start delousing both persons and bedding until even seasoned nurses had to call a halt for a spell.

Stirling Journal, 21 September 1939

1. *Make a list of the things which you think the evacuee was not used to.*
2. *What had surprised the 'frantic householders'?*

Bizzin Bees and Coos

Sometimes evacuees were unhappy in the country, away from home. The most difficult problem was the adults. Often they missed town life. Three ladies from Glasgow and their children were offered homes in the village of Garlogie.

When they got there they refused to leave the car which had taken them from the station. There was no cinema in the village. 'We dinna like bizzin bees and coos,' they said. They returned to Glasgow.

Aberdeen Press and Journal, May 1940

By January 1940 more than half of the evacuees had returned home; four out of every ten children, nine out of every ten adults. But the story of evacuation did not end then. Some of those who returned home in 1939 were evacuated again when the blitz began, or when there were rocket attacks on London in 1944. Some spent the whole war away from home.

Few were sorry to see the end of evacuation, but it did have one good result. More people became aware of the plight of the poor from Britain's cities. Townspeople saw that many villages still had no piped water. A few children learned that apples did not grow in boxes, and that cows were not the size of dogs.

Here is a letter one evacuee, Alan Skilton, wrote to his parents:

Dear Mum and Dad,

    I like the place and the people, but I would like to come home. I went to school today but I didn't like it so much as our school. When we got to the place, the teachers disappeared and didn't tell anything else except for telling us to go to school next week. I amused myself going to the fields or looking at books. I'm wearing my long socks but don't want to any more. Was it hot yesterday because it was here. We have no garden to play in. There is a girl living here. I wish I could come home.

    Your loving son Alan

1. Suggest two reasons why the ladies wished to return to Glasgow.
2. Look at the evacuee's letter again. Why do you think this boy wanted to go home?
3. What did the Government poster advise? Why?

(Now would be a good time to do Workguide 1.)

ISSUED BY THE MINISTRY OF HEALTH

3. Crisis

NAZIS INVADE HOLLAND, BELGIUM, LUXEMBURG: MANY AIRPORTS BOMBED

Blitzkrieg

The Bore War. That was what people were calling it by April 1940. Since the German attack on Poland in September 1939 nothing much seemed to have happened. There had been no heavy air-raids. No gas had been used. The war was becoming a nuisance. Then, suddenly, in the spring of 1940, all that changed. Look at the list of events on the right.

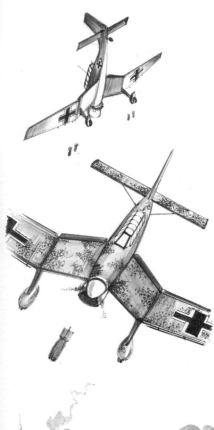

The weapons of lightning war: A Junkers 87B dive-bomber (Stuka) and Panzer Mark III tank. Stukas were successful in the early stages of the war, but proved too slow in the Battle of Britain.

April 9	Germans take Denmark and invade Norway
May 10	Germans invade Holland, Belgium and Luxemburg
May 13	Germans attack France at Sedan
May 15	Dutch surrender. Germans break through French defences at Sedan
May 20	Germans reach the Channel. Allied forces in Belgium and Northern France cut off
May 26	British and French troops trapped around Dunkirk. Day of prayer in Britain for safety of troops Evacuation from Dunkirk begins
May 28	Belgians surrender
June 4	Evacuation from Dunkirk ends
June 14	Germans enter Paris
June 17	French ask for a cease-fire
June 22	French surrender

1. Why do you think people talked of the 'Bore War' early in 1940?
2. List the European countries which fell to the Germans between April 9th and June 22nd.
3. How do you think these events affected: (a) the position of Britain in the war; (b) the attitude of the British people?

The speed of the German advance caught Europe by surprise. The pictures show the two weapons which had made this possible. This was *Blitzkrieg* - lightning war.

Dunkirk: Victory or Defeat?

A soldier who was there describes the scene on the beaches at Dunkirk:

The picture will always remain sharp-etched in my memory – the lines of men wearily and sleepily staggering across the beach from the dunes to the shallows, great columns of men thrust out into the water among the bomb and shell splashes. As the front ranks were dragged on board, the rear ranks moved up, from ankle deep to knee deep, from knee deep to waist deep, until they, too, came to shoulder depth and their turn.

A. D. Divine

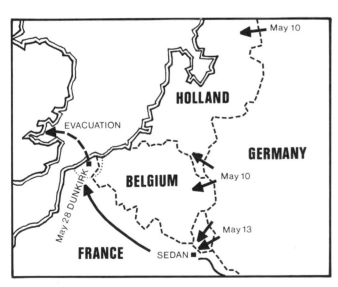

You will see Dunkirk on the map above. Around this town most of the British army were trapped along with French and Belgian troops. The harbour at Dunkirk was out of action. There seemed no escape for these men. They appeared to face certain death or capture. Yet, on May 26th, one of the most remarkable events of the war began - the attempt to rescue the British army from France. Code-named 'Operation Dynamo' the plan was for the Royal Navy and other smaller ships to bring the men away from the beaches at Dunkirk. Pleasure craft, ferries and fishing boats gathered in the Thames, then crossed to the beaches.

Dawn soon came. We stared at what looked like thousands of sticks on the beach and were amazed to see them turn into moving masses of humanity. I thought of going in, picking up seventy to eighty and clearing off. We got our load, so did the *Canvey Queen*, when I realised it would be selfish to clear off, when several destroyers and large vessels were waiting in deep water to be fed by small craft. So I decided what our job was to be.

Allan Barrell of the *Shamrock*

1. *Read the passages on this page and look at the pictures on this page and the next.*

   (a) *What had happened to the British army in France?*

Lucky enough to find transport from the beaches, these soldiers arrive at a waiting ship. Were they now safe?

(b) Describe in your own words the scene on the beaches.

2. What decision had the captain of the Shamrock made?

3. Why do you think the rescue of these men was so important?

For days the evacuation went on. Sometimes ships were damaged or sunk, but gradually the army was brought home. People on the south coast of England watched as the men came ashore. The *Daily Express* reported:

They were exhausted. They had not slept or eaten for days. Many tramped off in their stockinged feet. Others were in their shirt sleeves. Many had wounds. Many had torn uniforms.

The men came ashore in heaps, scarcely able to stand. I saw one man with a handkerchief over his head wound. Another with a torn trouser leg soaked in blood.

All night and day men and women, and even children, have been standing there with cups of tea, lumps of bread and cigarettes. They paid for them themselves. When their stocks ran out they sent schoolboys with barrows round the town appealing for help. The barrows came back piled with food and hundreds of cigarettes.

Above An artist's impression of the beaches at the height of the evacuation. Dunkirk burns in the background.

Below An army comes home. Note the French soldiers.

1. *What evidence is there that these troops had been under constant attack for days?*
2. *How would you describe the attitude of the people towards them?*

The evacuation ended on 4 June 1940. 338 226 men had been brought to safety. 40 000 British troops were left behind, dead or captured. An army had been saved. but it was an army without equipment.

Churchill

I have nothing to offer but blood, toil, tears and sweat. We have before us an ordeal of the most grievous kind. You ask 'What is our policy?' I will say it is to wage war, by sea, land and air, with all our might and with all the strength that God can give us. You ask 'What is our aim?' I can answer in one word: Victory – victory at all costs, victory in spite of all terror; victory, however long and hard the road may be; for without victory there is no survival.

Winston Churchill

Winston Churchill became Prime Minister on May 10th, the day on which the Germans attacked Holland and Belgium. Soon after, he made his first famous speech in the House of Commons. Part of it is printed above.

1. *What kind of person do you think Churchill was?*
2. *Do you think someone like Churchill would make a good Prime Minister at that time? Why?*

This poster shows Winston Churchill in a typical pose. Why do you think aircraft and tanks are shown in the background?

3. *Choose words or phrases from the speech which you think show:*
   (a) that the future would not be easy;
   (b) determination to fight on.

Churchill replaced Neville Chamberlain. Many people thought Chamberlain had been too half-hearted about the war. Churchill was very different. He had always spoken out against Hitler. He seemed a much stronger and more determined person. In the dark days of 1940 and 1941 he proved he could inspire the British to face the dangers and difficulties of the war.

(Now would be a good time to do Workguide 2.)

13

4. If the Invader Comes

Hitler surveys Paris, his most impressive conquest so far.

Britain Alone

Terrible news came on June 17th. The French had asked the Germans for a cease-fire. This meant they could not fight on. On June 22nd they finally surrendered. Britain was now alone against Germany. As the German army was preparing for a triumphal march through Paris, Hitler must have thought the war would soon be at an end. Surely Britain would make peace. Read what Churchill said as France collapsed:

The whole might and fury of the enemy must very soon be turned on us. Hitler knows that he will have to break us in this island or lose the war. If we can stand up to him, all Europe may be free. Let us therefore brace ourselves to our duties, and so bear ourselves that, if the British Empire and Commonwealth last for a thousand years, men will still say, 'This was their finest hour'.

1. *What would you say is the message of Churchill's speech and the cartoon on this page?*

Britain did not ask for peace. Hitler now prepared to invade Britain. 'Operation Sealion' was the name of his plan.

"VERY WELL, ALONE"

This Low cartoon in the *Evening Standard* summed up the attitude of many.

14

If the Invader Comes

Imagine living near the south coast of England in the summer of 1940. Everyone was expecting invasion. The question in people's minds was - where, when?

Newspapers and the radio were not free to tell the truth. No one could, therefore, be sure what might have happened. Rumours began to spread that German spies had landed by parachute. Some people were fined for spreading stories 'likely to lead to alarm and despondency'. Posters urged people not to gossip, or spread information that might be useful to an enemy. 'Careless Talk Costs Lives' was the message.

1. *Explain why the passengers in the cartoon are alarmed.*
2. *Look at the photograph on the right. Why would the road signs have been taken down?*

Church bells were not to be rung for services. They were only to be used by the army or the

police, as a sign of invasion. Signposts, station names - anything that might help an invader to find his way - were removed or blotted out. More important than any of these, however, was the need for more men to meet the invasion.

Uprooted road signs. How would they have helped invaders?

The Home Guard

On May 14th the call went out over the wireless. Volunteers between the age of 17 and 65 were needed to form the 'Local Defence Volunteers'. They would help the army defend the country. By July 1½ million men had volunteered. At first there were problems.

In Berkshire, one battalion received, as its first issue of arms, four rifles per one hundred men and only ten rounds per rifle. Pickaxes, crowbars, golf clubs, choppers or even dummy rifles which might bluff a paratrooper into submission, were taken out on the first patrols. One Lancashire battalion borrowed a quantity of rifles which had been used in the Crimean War and the Indian Mutiny; another provided each man with a six-foot [*nearly two metres*] spear.

A. Calder *The People's War 1939-45*

1. *What was the original name of the Home Guard?*
2. *What was its purpose?*
3. *What seems to have been a problem at first?*

This was the beginning of what we know as 'Dad's Army'. The name was changed from 'LDV' to 'Home Guard'. Its duties were to guard factories and airfields, and to watch for invasion. At first it was difficult to take the Home Guard seriously. Some men were rather old. One was still serving on his eightieth birthday and was presented with an ornamental clock. 'There is no truth in the rumour that our old friend, Private Taylor, fought at Bannockburn,' remarked the company commander.

N. Longmate *The Real Dad's Army*

1. *Why do you think the ceremony mentioned above might have been unique?*

As the months went by uniforms and weapons were provided, and training took place. The Home Guard staged an impressive march through London before it was disbanded in 1944. Looking back it is doubtful whether the Home Guard could have effectively resisted a German invasion. But they did leave the army free to concentrate on preparing for invasion, and there is no doubt that thousands of ordinary men in the Home Guard were prepared to have a go.

The Battle of Britain

Imagine that you could stand in your street, and watch a battle taking place. In the summer of 1940 people in the south of England could. Read what one newspaper reporter wrote:

I was one of hundreds of Londoners who stood in the streets cheering as two bombers were sent hurtling to destruction by our fighters yesterday. Thousands of feet above us we watched a terrific battle as fighters and bombers dodged in and out of the clouds. In a clear patch of blue sky I watched a bomber roar along with a fighter hard on its tail. Machine-guns rattled as the fighter swooped after it. For a few seconds we watched a thrilling air duel. Then the bomber almost stood on its nose in mid-air, came hurtling down in a death dive and blew up before it reached the ground. The pilot baled out and we watched him slowly glide down.

A. Hodgson, *Daily Herald*, 16 September 1940

1. *Which words or phrases describe the feelings of the watchers?*
2. *What dangers would there be for these people?*

Hitler and Hermann Goering were confident. Goering commanded the German air force (the *Luftwaffe*). Because Britain would not surrender, he had been ordered to destroy the R.A.F. After that the invasion of Britain - Operation Sealion - would be able to go ahead. The main German attacks came in August and September, 1940. Over the south coast of England the Hurricane and Spitfire pilots of the R.A.F. took on the bombers and fighters of the *Luftwaffe*. This was the 'Battle of Britain'. Boys re-enacted it in school playgrounds, arms outstretched. Newspapers reported the numbers of aircraft lost as if they were cricket scores. '185 for 26' was one day's headline. We now know that only 60 German planes were destroyed that day.

1. *What do you think 185 for 26 meant?*
2. *Try to think of reasons why the success of the R.A.F. was often exaggerated in Britain.*
3. *Would it have been better for papers to underestimate the R.A.F.'s success? Why?*

On 12 October 1940 Hitler cancelled Operation Sealion. Goering had failed in his promise to destroy the R.A.F. The invasion scare was over. Winston Churchill summed up the thoughts of many when he said of the Battle of Britain fighter pilots:

Never in the field of human conflict was so much owed by so many to so few.

But the pilots were not the only ones who deserved praise. There were the 'forgotten ones' too, the ground crews, the repair units, the control stations, radar operators, the Royal Observer Corps and many others.

The *Luftwaffe* now turned its attention to the bombing of London. Perhaps that would force Britain out of the war.

1. *Why do you think we call the battle between the R.A.F. and the Luftwaffe the* Battle of Britain?

(This would be a good time to do Workguide 3.)

This scene looks peaceful as pilots rest before a Hawker Hurricane fighter, but danger or death might be only minutes away.

Messerchmitt Bf 109s. German bombers were no match for RAF fighters in the Battle of Britain, but the ME Bf 109 fighter escorts were worthy opponents for Spitfires and Hurricanes.

5. The Blitz

> Mummy, stop singing,
> I can't hear the bombs.

London in Flames

The first wave of German bombers was spotted heading for London one Saturday afternoon. Just before 5 pm on 7 September 1940 sirens gave the warning - two minutes of the wavering note. The blitz was about to begin.

The last bombers did not leave until around 4.30 the following morning. For the next nine months they were to return many times. Other towns, too, would discover the horror of being bombed.

1. *Look at the picture. You can see German bombers over London on September 7th.*
   (a) *Is it a daytime or night-time raid?*
   (b) *Do you think these bombers would be able to hit targets accurately?*

The morning after that first night of the blitz, an American broadcaster living in London told what he had seen:

We drove back to the East End of London. It was like an obstacle race. Streets were roped off, houses and shops smashed. Three red buses were drawn up in a line waiting to take away the homeless. Men were leading dull-eyed women across to the buses. Most of them were carrying cheap little suitcases and sometimes bulging paper bags. That was all they had left.

Edward R. Murrow (adapted)

The *blitz* is the name we give to the time between 7 September 1940 and 10 May 1941, when German bombers made mass attacks against British towns. Bombs fell on Britain before and after that time, but the blitz was the worst period. At first bombing was carried out in daylight as well as at night. Soon, however, the bombers came only at night.

1. *What kind of night would suit the bomber pilots best?*
2. *Can you think why they stopped coming in daylight?*

Exploding bombs were not the only danger. Thousands of fire-bombs (incendiaries) were also dropped. They did not explode, but were intended to become lodged in roofs, beginning fires. One night - 29 December 1940 - fire bombs began 1400 fires in the centre of London. The city centre became a raging inferno.

1. *Do you think fire-bombs were as dangerous as high-explosive ones? Why?*

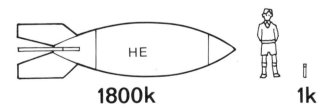

1800k   **1k**

People learned how to put out fire-bombs before they could cause damage. Even children could put out fire-bombs. 'Fire-watchers' were appointed to watch for bombs landing on roofs, and to put out fires there before they could spread.

From Coventry to Clydebank

The night of 14 November 1940 will always be remembered in Coventry. That night the bombers made a surprise attack there. 554 people were killed, 50 000 houses, hundreds of shops and the Cathedral were all destroyed. The citizens of Coventry were stunned. Two visitors described what they saw the next day:

As we came to the edge of the city, the air became as warm as a spring day. Though it was noon, the city was darkened by the black fog that clouded the sky and the thick banks of soot that were suspended over the streets. The people who walked the streets had grimy faces and their eyes were reddened with the heat and smoke.

Hilde Marchant *Women and Children Last*

Above Many auxiliary firemen assisted the Fire Brigades during the blitz. Here firemen risk the bombs to tackle a blaze.

Left High explosive (HE) bombs could be of many sizes. Fire bombs were only a few centimetres long, but could be more damaging.

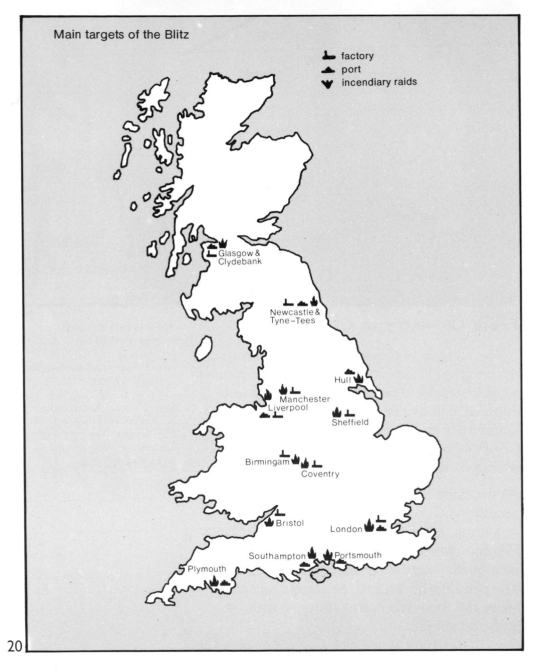

Main targets of the Blitz

factory
port
incendiary raids

Glasgow &
Clydebank

Newcastle &
Tyne-Tees

Hull

Manchester
Liverpool

Sheffield

Birmingam
Coventry

Bristol

London

Southampton   Portsmouth

Plymouth

A few miles outside Coventry I met the first large group of refugees. Children were being carried in their fathers' arms, and pushed along in prams. There were suitcases and bundles on people's shoulders; little families trudged along hand in hand, with rugs, blankets, and anything they could save from their ruined homes. I saw several people making preparations to lie down under hedgerows.

Daily Herald 16 November 1940

1. *What evidence is there (a) that there had been many fires in Coventry, and (b) that many houses had been destroyed?*
2. *Where do you think the people described in the Daily Herald were going, and why?*
3. *Study the map, and try to explain why Coventry was bombed.*

Notice that even one raid on a smaller town could seem worse than the more frequent attacks on London. This was the case in March 1941, when the raiders struck Glasgow and Clydeside. The worst nights there were 13 and 14 March. The houses and tenements of Clydeside were more densely packed than those of English towns.

Houses, churches, schools and other buildings in the area were wrecked. In this district, hardly a pane of glass remained in houses or shops. Streets were strewn with broken glass, rubble and debris. The people of the blitzed districts spent yesterday recovering property and furniture from partially [*partly*] ruined homes and settling down in new billets, while a few had the task of tracing missing relatives.

Glasgow Herald, 15 March, 1941

In Clydebank only seven out of 12000 houses remained undamaged. Fortunately, most of the inhabitants had not been there. Many had taken to the moors behind the town, spending the night as best they could. By day they might return to jobs or home.

1. *Why was the damage to houses in Clydebank greater than in English towns?*
2. *From what you have read and seen of the blitz, what do you think would be the most urgent tasks to be done (a) during, and (b) after an air-raid?*

(Now would be a good time to do Workguide 4.)

Though bombed houses were quickly repaired, many people were homeless for a time. One man pushes away salvaged belongings.

6. Shelters

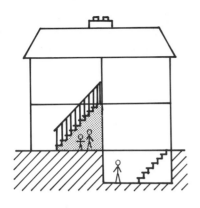

Where to shelter at home. These were the safest places in a house.

An Anderson shelter like this provided protection from anything but a direct hit. Some people, however, preferred to stay in the house.

When the Siren Goes, Take Cover

Most people sheltered from the bombs in their own homes or gardens. The pictures show how this could be done.

1. *Which were the safest parts of a house? Why?*
2. *What name was given to the garden shelter? Why would many families not have these?*
3. *Which way of sheltering would be (a) safest, and (b) most comfortable?*

By September 1940 2 ¼ million Andersons had been issued. You had to erect them yourself, and put in fittings. They were to be placed in a hole dug in the garden and covered over with 15 inches of soil. The two descriptions below help us to picture what the blitz was like for ordinary folk, in their homes and shelters.

Had our meal, I washed up and about to do night jobs when the raid got very fierce. We did a bunk to shelter, dog not walked either. Terrific noise. We tired and went to sleep. I woke up about 10.30 pm and heard six bombs. Pretty close by sound. Went to sleep again. Gunfire and noise terrific after midnight. Only dozed. Then after 1 am, swish, swish, all over the place. We crawled out hastily. None near us but all the sky behind us brilliant from many incendiaries.

Les said 'Dinner or no dinner we're going down to the shelter, I hope you've bailed it out.' We scrambled into our clothes, carried a blanket and cushions and hoped for the best. The sky was one blaze of light, gunfire was going on and did we run!

We all got in safely, the floor was one large puddle. We sorted ourselves out and made the best of it.

Mass Observation Archive

1. *What evidence is there that Anderson shelters were (a) wet, (b) cold, and (c) noisy?*
2. *What were incendiaries? How did the family in the first passage know incendiaries were falling?*
3. *Why do you think they were worried by incendiaries?*

In the Tube

In crowded parts of towns many families did not have their own shelter. They could go to street shelters, made of brick and concrete. These were not popular. They were cold and dark, with wooden benches and chemical toilets. People did not think they would be safe. Some Londoners found a better way to shelter:

October 24th was a cold, damp, windy day. People began queueing at daylight. There were hundreds there when the station doors opened at 3.30 pm. By 4 o'clock the platforms were all staked out. Most people had reserved places for friends or relatives. There were arguments about places, but eventually everything settled down. Late arrivals, after 8 pm, had to sleep at the top of the emergency stairs. Although it was stuffy and sanitation was primitive, there was a feeling of security at being with others, and you couldn't hear the bombs.

Mass Observation Archive

1. *What kind of station was used for sheltering?*
2. *What belongings have the people in the picture taken with them?*
3. *Why do you think some families preferred the underground stations to other shelters?*
4. *Some people accused the tube shelterers of being cowards. What do you think?*

Even in the 'Tube' there could be danger. In October 1940 a bomb fell above Balham station,

These Tube-shelterers in Holborn were lucky to have bunks. At first everyone had to sleep on the platforms.

killing 64 and injuring 550 of those sheltering below.

Men and Women of the A.R.P.

When bombs fell, houses were destroyed and damaged. People were killed or injured. Others were trapped. During a raid, the Police and the Fire Service came into action, and so did the A.R.P., who were part-time volunteers. A.R.P. stands for Air Raid Precautions. The best known members of the A.R.P. were the Air Raid Wardens, but others, too, played an important part. There were the Rescue, First Aid and Stretcher Parties, and Ambulance drivers.

23

11 January 1941. Clearing rubble from Bank Underground Station which had been hit.

"Give him my compliments, and tell him that while we admire the subtlety of his point, we prefer to assume that the black-out regulations do *not* apply to search-lights . . ."

1. The Wardens' tasks were to report damage and fires in their own area to the A.R.P. Centre. What would be the jobs of the other A.R.P. services mentioned on page 23?
2. What dangers do you think A.R.P. men, and others like the Fire and Police services, would face during the blitz?

At first, before the bombing began, the Wardens were treated as something of a joke. 'Three quid a week's too much for just playing cards and such like' was one comment on the A.R.P. All wardens also had the unpopular duty of checking to see that blackout rules were being enforced.

1. *Suggest two reasons why the A.R.P., and Wardens in particular, were unpopular at first.*

Once the blitz began, the A.R.P. workers became heroes rather than figures of fun. Sometimes there were dramatic rescues. In Wallasey in March 1941 bombs destroyed a house. A man and his wife were killed, but no one else could be found. Three days later Rescue men were searching the rubble. They heard a cry below them. Could it be a cat? Digging down carefully, they came across a baby only weeks old. She had survived for over three days, and was brought to safety.

The Second Blitz

The blitz was a frightening time. It ended in May 1941. The bombing had not crippled Britain, nor had it destroyed the spirit of the people.

In 1944 there came a new danger. The Germans began to use new weapons to attack London. First came the 'flying bombs' - the V1s. These were small pilotless aircraft (about 7 metres long). At one time over 100 a day were reaching Britain, but they could be caught by aircraft or shot down. Later in 1944 the V2s appeared. They were rockets (about 14 metres long), which travelled at 3000 miles an hour - faster than sound. There was no way to shoot them down. There could be no warning. For a time London suffered another blitz in 1944. Children were evacuated, the A.R.P. were in action, shelters were in use. Fortunately Germany was invaded before long. The last bomb - a V1 - fell on Britain in March 1945.

1. *People were often more afraid of V2s than V1s (doodlebugs). Why?*

(Now would be a good time to do Workguide 5.)

7. At Home in Wartime

Britain's Life Line

Britain is a small country. British industries depend on raw materials from abroad. In wartime supplies were needed urgently to make weapons of war. It was the job of the merchant navy to bring these supplies, and take the finished weapons to the army wherever it was fighting.

The Germans knew how important to Britain her merchant ships were. From the beginning of the war they attacked them with submarines and warships. Over 5000 ships were sunk. The job of merchant seaman was one of the most dangerous of the war.

The rafts had drifted for 15 days during which time seven of the men had died. Then a convoy was sighted. On the bosun's suggestion, a tobacco tin was tied to the end of a long-handled scoop to reflect the sun's rays and attract attention. Only one man had the strength to wave the pole.

A steamship company's report (adapted)

I. What do you think had happened to these men?

To give ships some protection, convoys were organised. Groups of ships sailed together, escorted by ships of the Royal Navy, and part of the way by aircraft as well. Sometimes the

A convoy under attack.

Navy could not spare ships for escort duty; then armed merchant ships would protect the convoy. A convoy might bring over £100 000 000 worth of supplies. You can see some of the items one convoy brought listed here.

Wheat	Guns	Sugar
Timber	Flax	Copper
Aluminium	Tank parts	Cotton
Cheese	Shells	Orange juice
Motor trucks	Bombs	Landing craft
Steel alloy	TNT	
Chemicals	Dried fruit	

I. Make three lists from the goods carried by the convoy:
(a) raw materials for the factories;
(b) finished goods for the war;
(c) foods.

With enough U-Boats we can and will finish off the British Isles.
(*Admiral Doenitz, 1941*)

Ration book and identity card.

In 1941 every adult was entitled to this amount of rationed food.

 8oz (226g) Fat (including 2oz butter)

 **2oz (57g) Tea**

2 slices cooked meat

 4oz (114g) Ham

 1oz (28g) Cheese

 8oz (226g) Sugar

2oz (57g) Jam

 **1s. (5p) worth of meat**

 1 Egg

2. *Why do you think space was found for food at such a time?*
3. *Why was the merchant navy so important to Britain?*
4. *There are many exciting stories about merchantmen at war. One concerns the Jervis Bay. Find out what happened.*

Rationing

If you dropped an egg in the street, you would not dream of scraping it up and carrying it home. During the war at least one woman did. Another remembers seeing a dog run out of a butcher's shop with a large piece of suet in its mouth. She followed on her bicycle. The dog buried the suet, and then:

When the dog was safely away I went to the spot and confiscated the hidden treasure. I took that suet home, cut out the mauled part and then made suet pudding.

Longmate How We Lived Then

1. *Why do you think these women did these things?*

Food was in short supply in wartime. Britain did not produce enough of certain essential foods to feed all her people. That is why ships carried food as well as war supplies; but less food could be carried than before the war.

To make sure that everyone got a fair share of scarce food, the Government introduced rationing in January 1940. Everyone was issued with a ration book. The coupons in the book allowed you to buy a certain amount of rationed food each week. The diagram on the left shows one person's ration for a week in 1941 - the worst time of shortage.

Remember that not all food was rationed. Some foods were plentiful, like potatoes, carrots, onions and bread. Some were scarce but unrationed, like fish and fruit. Some were almost impossible to get, like fresh oranges and bananas. Dried eggs and dried milk from America were not rationed, and helped to make up for shortages.

1. *Why was there a shortage of some food in wartime?*
2. *What might have happened if there had been no rationing?*
3. *How do you think rationing would affect (a) the rich, and (b) the poor?*

Rationing was a nuisance, but it was not unpopular. People could understand that it was necessary and fair. You may think the amount of rations shown in the picture on page 26 looks very small, but together with unrationed food, it was enough to keep a person perfectly healthy. Some people were entitled to extra rations — pregnant women, children and manual workers.

It may seem strange, but it was discovered that children were healthier in wartime than they had been before. There was less disease, and poor children, in particular, were better nourished.

1. *Why do you think the Government urged people to eat more carrots and potatoes?*
2. *Who was entitled to extra rations? Can you suggest why?*
3. *Why do you think some children were healthier at the time of rationing than before?*

Digging for Victory

'Let "dig for victory" be the motto of everyone with a garden,' said the Government Minister on the radio. One way to help the war effort was to grow more food. Gardeners began to plant more vegetables, and more people began to cultivate allotments.

Some were more ambitious. They might keep pigs, goats, cows or bees. Sometimes a street would form a 'pig club', feeding their own pig from scraps of food. Another way to provide more fresh food was to keep hens or rabbits. You could eat the eggs and, later, the hens too. One woman remembers keeping hens:

A new use for the moat of the Tower of London.
Find out which spaces near you were turned into allotments.

Soon the first precious egg was in my hands, more precious to me than the crown jewels, and it had a double yolk.

Longmate *How We Lived Then*

The hen that laid the double yolk egg soon died, and was buried in the garden!

Local councils ploughed up parkland and playing fields. Golf Clubs had to plough up part of their courses - or graze sheep. Even railway embankments were dug over.

1. *Would you eat any rabbits or hens that you kept?*
2. *Why might neighbours complain about people keeping rabbits or hens?*

every available piece of land must be cultivated

GROW YOUR OWN FOOD

On the Farm

Some grumbled about the farmers. One person noticed:

Farmers were as poor as church mice, but before the war was half over they had not one but two cars in their garage. It made most of them. The government was generosity itself.

Longmate *How We Lived Then*

1. *What does the comment above suggest about farmers?*
2. *Do you think it was likely to be true? Why?*

Probably most farmers did eat more eggs, butter and meat than other people, but if they were better off they certainly had to work for their money. Before the war the prices for farm produce had been low. Farmers had no encouragement to produce more. Now the Government ordered more to be grown. More land was to be ploughed up. More wheat, barley, oats and potatoes were to be sown, and more dairy cattle kept. The Government bought at a fixed price everything a farmer could produce.

All this meant hard work for the farmers and their families. One farmer used to plough in winter by the light of the moon. Remember that in those days there was less farm machinery than today. Many of the jobs, especially harvesting and milking, were done without combines or milking machines. Some farms still used horses rather than tractors.

Nevertheless, the farmers were winning the battle for food. Compared with 1939, twice as much wheat and potatoes were being grown by 1944.

1. *Why would growing more crops and keeping more dairy cattle mean harder work for farmers?*
2. *Would farms in those days need more or fewer workers than today? How might the war pose a problem for farmers?*

Make Do and Mend

Some things were hard to do without. Everything that had been taken for granted in peacetime was now in short supply. The Government ordered factories to make war supplies, so that only a small amount of other goods could be made.

One of the most annoying shortages was of clothing. In 1941 clothes became rationed, rather like food. Each person was entitled to 66 clothing coupons a year. You can see on page 29 how many coupons different items of clothing required. Remember you still had to pay as well.

1. *Work out the coupon value of the clothes you came to school in. What would you have left from your year's supply of coupons?*
2. *How do you think clothes rationing would affect attitudes to worn-out clothes, second-hand clothes and hand-me-downs?*

It was important to save material. The Government ordered that men's jackets should be made single-breasted only, with no more than three pockets. Trousers were not to have turn-ups, and their legs were not to be wider than 19 inches [about 27cm] at the bottom. One tailor was fined for making an illegal pair of trousers with turn-ups! Boys under 12 could only be bought short trousers.

Probably young women were hardest hit. They would care more about how they were dressed. Perhaps they would want to wear something different to a dance or the pictures. Stockings and make-up were difficult to get, too. One woman dyed her legs with onion skins and another stained hers with gravy browning, to look like stockings.

Women became expert at turning any material they could find into new clothes. Table-cloths, curtains, blackout material, furniture covering, even coffin lining and parachute silk - all found its way to the sewing machine. One mother made a child's coat from old chamois leather!

1. Why do you think it was forbidden to sell trousers with turn-ups?

2. If you decided to go out with gravy browning on your legs, why would it be as well to check the weather forecast?

3. Some schools still insisted on full school uniform in wartime. What difficulties would that pose for families? (Note: Clothing coupons could be used for anyone in the family.)

4. The sign on the right appeared on wartime clothes and furniture. Find out what it meant.

(Now would be a good time to do Workguide 6.)

A shop assistant prepares to cut out clothing coupons.

	Coupons	
Hat	–	
Scarf	2	2
Coat	11	14
Cardigan	3	5
Woollen Dress	8	11
Petticoat	3	4
Slip	3	4
Other underwear	2	3
Handkerchiefs	1	1
Gloves	2	2
Ankle socks	1	1
Shoes	3	5
		Adults

	Coupons	
Cap	–	
Scarf	2	2
Shirt	6	8
Tie	1	1
Pullover	3	5
Overcoat	11	16
Vest	2	4
Shorts	3	5
Pants	2	4
Gloves	2	2
Long Trousers	6	8
Socks	1	3
Shoes	3	7
		Adults

Coupon values for children's clothes compared with those for adults (in second column).

Left, left,
you had a good job
and you left.

8. At Work

The 'call-up' began with the younger men. The Government ordered that they should report to their local Labour Exchange. First they had to register, then have a medical examination. If they were fit, and not doing a job which was considered essential, they would have to join one of the armed forces. Eventually all men between 18 and 41 were registered. This was the 'call-up' or conscription. It was to make sure that there were fit men for the forces, and that those doing important work should stay at their jobs.

1. *What jobs do you think would be considered 'essential' in wartime?*
2. *If you had been a young man then, would you have preferred to join the forces or remain at work?*

Mining, engineering, shipbuilding, the aircraft industry, railways, the merchant navy, police, firemen, building workers, scientists and lighthouse keepers were some essential workers. One of the most important groups was the coal miners. Coal was needed for industry, yet there were not enough miners. Men could choose mining rather than the forces when registering, but very few did, Eventually, in 1943, the Minister of Labour, Ernest Bevin, ordered that one conscript in every ten should be sent to the mines. These reluctant miners became known as 'Bevin Boys'.

1. *Why do you think mining was not a popular choice with conscripts?*
2. *Do you consider miners and other essential workers did as much for the war effort as those who entered the forces? Why?*

Women's Work

One man recalls that his sister's hands were pitted with sharp metal splinters and covered in oil sores. This woman was working in a munitions factory [making ammunition]. She was one of thousands who took up work during the war, to make up for the shortage of men. Women worked in munitions, engineering and

Another use for a Tube tunnel at Redbridge. The Plessey Company made electronic equipment.

chemicals. They worked on buses and as postwomen, and in many other jobs. Wartime work was hard, and hours were long. At one time it was usual for men to work 60 hours a week, and women 55 hours. For some young women this made a very full day.

The two girls were up before 6, to leave home at 6.30. They had a long walk to catch the special factory bus at 7.10, and after working an eleven-hour day, were lucky to catch the 7.30 pm bus back from town. They arrived home with only time for a quick meal, wash and change before going out dancing or to the pictures.

Longmate *How We Lived Then*

1. *Why was there a need for women to work in wartime?*
2. *How would women's work affect family incomes?*

The Land Army

Being in the Women's Land Army could be hard. One Land Girl remembers:

Once on a bitter day, when we were kicking parsnips out of the frozen earth, a colleague appeared in a long A.R.P. coat, reaching from ears to ankles. Against the background of powdered snow, bare trees and frozen landscape, she reminded me of a figure from the film 'Napoleon's Retreat from Moscow'.

Longmate *How We Lived Then*

The Land Girls were all volunteers. There were 90 000 of them by 1943, working on Britain's farms. The Land Girls spread muck, milked cows, harvested, dug vegetables out of frozen winter ground, trained as ratcatchers, and still managed to enjoy the work.

1. *Many of the Land Girls came from towns. Why do you think they volunteered?*
2. *The Land Army was often last to be considered for supply of uniforms, boots, etc. Was that fair?*
3. *You can see a Land Girl in uniform in the poster. Was the uniform (a) attractive, and (b) sensible?*

(Now would be a good time to do Workguide 7.)

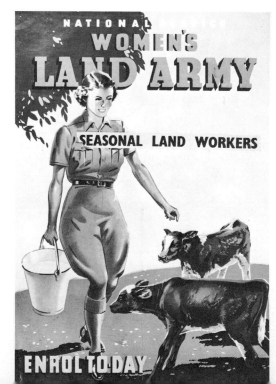

Radio Programmes

FORCES
(296.1m, 342.1m)
6.30 A.M.—News, Records.
7.00—News; Records.
8.00—News.
8.15—Records.
9.00—News; Records.
10.00—Mail Call.
10.30—Albert Sandler's Orch.
11.15—G. Thalben-Ball (Organ).
11.30—West Kent's Band.
12 noon—News.
12.10—Service.
12.40—Records.
1.00—News.
1.15—Lou Preager's Orch.
2.00—News; Northern Orch.
2.30—India Command.
3.00—News; Forces Favourites.
3.30—Radio Newsreel.
3.45—Scottish Orch.
4.50—War Review.
5.00—News.
5.15—Harry Fryer's Orch.

6.00—Light Music.
6.05—S. African News Letter.

6.15—Navy Mixture.
7.00—News.
7.15—Forces Favourites.
8.00—Old Town Hall.
8.30—Questions Answered.
9.00—News; Jack Payne's Parade.
9.50—Doris Arnold: Records.
10.30—Richard Crean's Orch.
10.50—News.

HOME
(203.3m, 391.1m, 449.1m)
7. A.M.—News.
7.15—Exercises.
7.30—Records.
7.55—Prayer.
8.00—News.
8.15—Kitchen Front.
8.30—Maritza Players.
9.00—Records.
9.15—Breton and Cornish Songs.
10.05—Schools.
10.15—Service.
10.30—BBC Variety Orch.
11.00—Schools.
12 noon—BBC Orch.

12.30—Workers' Playtime.
1.00—News.
1.15—Home on the Range.
1.40—Topical Magazine.
2.00—Schools.
3.00—Coventry Hippodrome Orch.
3.30—Opera's Older Generation;
    Records.
4.15—The Dansant.
5.00—News and Service in Welsh.
5.20—Children.
6.00—News.
6.30—Talk.
6.45—Hawaiian Music; Records.
7.00—Farming Today.
7.20—BBC Orch.
8.00—Travellers' Tales.
8.30—Tommy Handley in 'Itma'.

9.00—Big Ben; Minute for Reflection; News.
9.25—War Commentary.
9.40—'Dinner with a Novelist' (play).
10.10—Service.
10.30—Poems about Trades.
10.15—Colin Horsley (piano).
11.20—Stanley Black's Dance Orch.
12 midnight—News.

9. At Play

What shall we do tonight?

There was no television in wartime. In those days the wireless provided news and entertainment at home. Look at the programmes for one wartime day on the left. The programmes marked 'Forces' were for the armed forces, those marked 'Home' were the normal programmes.

1. *What word do most people use nowadays instead of wireless?*
2. *What was on the Home Service at 8.15 am, 8.30 pm and 9.25 pm?*
3. *Why do you think people would listen carefully to news broadcasts?*

Notice that apart from news programmes, most others were music or light entertainment. One of the most popular comedy programmes was ITMA, which stood for 'It's That Man Again', starring Tommy Handley.

In September 1939 all public places like cinemas and football grounds were closed, but they soon re-opened. People wanted to enjoy their evenings despite the war. During the blitz, some people refused to leave the cinema when the air-raid warning went, so they could see the end of the film. You can see advertisements for some popular wartime films on this page. You

may recognise the names of some of the film stars who were famous then.

Dancing was also popular in wartime. One girl wrote in her diary:

October 17th. Dance at the Village Hall. Packed out with airmen. Some were our own. Some were American. Had a very good time. Seen home by a very nice American called Dave.

Quoted in Reynoldson *The War at Home*

1. *Why do you think dances and the cinema were popular, even during the blitz?*
2. *Can you suggest why American servicemen were popular with British girls?*

American servicemen were paid more than the British forces. They were able to get more cigarettes, and sometimes even nylon stockings which were very scarce in wartime Britain. Perhaps British girls thought they were like the American film stars they saw in films. However, the Americans were not always so popular with British men!

Brighton 0 Norwich 18

You would be unlikely to come across a football score like this today. It happened during the war. Brighton could only field five players. They managed to scrape together a team with the help of two Norwich reserves, and five soldiers from the crowd!

1. *See if you can predict how the war affected*

The Rainbow Room in London was a popular meeting place for American servicemen.

sport, by thinking about these questions:
(a) *How might war affect football players, grounds, leagues?*
(b) *What sort of sports or games would be most affected, and least? Football? Cricket? Golf? Fishing?*
(c) *How might the war have affected your local public park or sports ground?*
Read below to see whether your predictions were correct.

Football was completely reorganised. To save time and travelling new leagues began. In England there were 'Southern', 'Western' and 'Northern' Leagues. You can see some results for one Saturday on page 34.

ALL YESTERDAY'S FOOTBALL

INTERNATIONAL MATCH
Half-time scores in parentheses.

ENGLAND (1).....6   SCOTLAND (1)....2
30,000—Hagan 2,   Dodds 2
Macaulay o.g.,
Lawton, Mercer,
Carter
(At Wembley.)

LEAGUE SOUTH CUP

ARSENAL (4).....7   LUTON (1)........1
D Compton 4,   Goodyear
Drake 4
BRENTFORD (2)..3   C PALACE (2).....4
Townsend 2,   Girling, Ferrier 2,
Stevens   J Lewis
BRIGHTON (0)..1   CHARLTON (2)....2
Longdon   Welsh, Embleton
CHELSEA (1)....3   S'THAMPT'N (2)..2
Payne (pen),   Whittingham 2
Mitten, Tennant
C ORIENT (0)....2   Q.P.R. (5).......5
Smith, Sharpe   Swinfen 2, Burley
2, Sidley
MILLWALL (0)...0   TOTTENH'M (0)..1
Beasley
(At Selhurst Park.)
P'TSMOUTH (0)..0   ALDERSHOT (2)..2
Morris, Powell
READING (2).....3   FULHAM (0).......0
Hopper, Bradley,
McPhee
WEST HAM (0)..1   WATFORD (1)....2
Weaver   W Brown 2

Scottish Southern.—Airdrie (0) 2 Third
Lanark (1) 3—Clyde (0) 0 Morton (2) 3—
Dumbarton (1) 2 Hearts (0) 1—Falkirk
(2) 3 St Mirren (0) 0—Hibs (2) 2 Partick
(0) 0—Motherwell (0) 1 Celtic (2) 2—
Queen's Pk (1) 2 Hamilton (1) 3—Rangers
(2) 5 Albion R (0) 0.
Scottish N.E.—Dundee U (2) 3 E Fife (0)
1—Dunfermline (0) 1 Rangers (1) 3—
Hearts (1) 1 Aberdeen (1) 2—Raith R (1)
3 Falkirk (1) 1.

LEAGUE NORTH CUP.—Qualifying Competition

BATH C (1)........3   SWANSEA (0)....0
McCulloch, Little,
Rosenthal
BIRM'GHAM (1)..1   A VILLA (0).......1
Trigg   Iverson
BLACKPOOL (1)..2   ROCHDALE (0)...0
Dix (pen),
H O'Donnell
BOLTON (3).......5   SOUTHPORT (0)..1
Currier 4,   Smith
Middlesbrough
BRADFORD (1)...3   BARNSLEY (3)...3
Horsman 2, Ainsley   Shotton, Asquith 2
BRISTOL C (1)....2   ABERAMAN (0)...0
Norcott,
Hargreaves
BURNLEY (3).....5   BLACKBURN (0)..0
Brocklebank 4,   Aspen
Watson
CARDIFF (1).....2   LOVELL'S (0).....0
Wood, Low o.g.
CHEST'FLD (1)..5   GRIMSBY (0).....1
Milburn 2 (2   Pearson
pen), Kidd,
Linacre 2
COVENTRY (1)..2   N'AMPTON (0)...0
Dennison o.g.,
Lowrie
DERBY (0).........0   MANSFIELD (1)..1
Smith
DONCASTER (0)..1   SHEFF UTD (2)..3
Massarella   Thompson, Pickering
HALIFAX (2).....3   MAN CITY (2)....2
Fisher, Smith 2   Heale 2, Doherty,
Williamson 2
HARTLEP'LS (2)..3   GATESHEAD (2).
Short 2, Small—   Turnbull, Forster
2, Johnson 2,
Harrison
BRADF'RD C

LEAGUE SOUTH CUP (continued)

LEEDS (1).........2   YORK (1)..........1
Mahon, Henry   Hawkins
LINCOLN (1)....2   ROTHERH'M (1)..4
Lello, Lowrey   Ardron 2, Barton,
Austin
LIVERPOOL (1)..4   CHESTER (1)....2
Done, Nieuwen-   Yates, Hughes
huys, Campbell,
Liddell
MAN UTD (1)....3   OLDHAM (0)......2
Smith 3   Taylor (pen),
Cotterill
N'CASTLE (0)...2   DARL'NGT'N (0)..0
Stubbins 2 (1 pen)
NOTTM F (0).....1   LEICESTER (0)...0
Johnston
SHEFF WED (1)..2   NOTTS CO (0)...0
Cockcroft (pen),
Wright
STOCKPORT (2)..5   BURY (1)..........1
Talbot, Worsley,   Robinson
Shaw, Catterick
SUND'LAND (0)..3   MIDD'SBRO (0)..0
...sidman, Has-

Soccer Summary

INTERNATIONAL.—England 2, Wales 2
(at Liverpool)

LEAGUE SOUTH.—Aldershot 1, Orient 0;
Brighton 1, Fulham 3; Chelsea 8, Palace 2;
Luton 1, Brentford 7; Millwall 5,
J; Q.P.R. 6, West Ham 1; Southampton 0,
Arsenal 2; Tottenham 1, Portsmouth 0; Wat-
ford 2, Reading 2.

LEAGUE WEST.—Aberaman 0, Bristol C.
4; Bath 2, Cardiff 2; Lovell's 5, Swansea 0.

LEAGUE NORTH.—Accrington 2, Bradford
C. 3; Villa 3, Wolves 0; Barnsley 2, Bradford
Bolton 1, Blackpool 0; Bradford 1, Newcastle
0; Burnley 3, Southport 1; Bury 1, Everton
4; Coventry 0, Birmingham 1; Crewe 0,
Tranmere 1; Darlington 2, Hartlepools 1;
Gateshead 5, Middlesbrough 2; Grimsby 2, Man-
Doncaster 1, Hull 2, Halifax 0; Lincoln 0,
Chesterfield 1; Manchester C. 2, Liverpool
2; Northampton 1, Stoke 1; Nottm. For. 2,
Sheffield U. 2; Port Vale 0, West Bromwich
0; Preston 4, Oldham 1; Rochdale 2, Blackburn 0; Rotherham 0, Mansfield 0; Sheffield
Wed 6, Notts Co. 1; Stockport 4, Manchester U. 4; Sunderland 5, Leeds 1; Walsall
0, Leicester 1; Wrexham 1, Chester 1; York
1, Huddersfield 3

SCOTTISH SOUTHERN LEAGUE.—Albion
R. 2, Motherwell 0; Clyde 5, Falkirk 1;
Hamilton 3, St. Mirren 1; Hearts 4, Third
Lanark 1; Morton 2, Partick 0; Queens Park
0, Hibernian 2; Rangers 2, Airdrie 0; Dum-
barton 0, Celtic 3.

SCOTTISH N.E. LEAGUE.—Arbroath 1,
Dundee 4; Dundee U. 3, Rangers 0; Raith R.
3, Hearts 0; East Fife 5, Aberdeen 4; Falkirk 0, Dunfermline 3.

OTHER MATCH.—Norwich 9, R A F XI 1.

AMATEUR MATCHES.— Herts and
Middlesex League: Barnet 4, Wealdstone 2;
Grays 1, Finchley 7; St Albans 2, Golders
Green 3; Southall 5, Clapton 3; Tufnell Park
2, Walthamstow Av. 0; Wood Green 0,
Hitchin 1; Slough 7, Leyton 0. S.E. Com-
bination Cup (1st Rd.): LFF 5, Bromley
1; Topping and Mitcham 0, Sutton 4; Epsom
1, Walton-on-Thames 0; Erith and Belve-
dere 1, Gravesend 2.

RUGBY UNION.—Wasps 33, Streatham 3;
Newport 35, R A F 0.

ENGLAND'S LIKELY TEAM
By FRANK COLES

England's team to meet Scotland at
Wembley on Feb. 19 will probably be
announced to-day. No radical changes
are anticipated in the side which
played Wales in the autumn. Spurs,
Ditchburn, of the 'Spurs, may win a
new 'cap' in goal. The probable
eleven is:
Ditchburn (Tottenham); Scott (Arsenal),
Hardwick (Middlesbrough); Britton (Everton),
Cullis (Wolves), Mercer (Everton); Lawton
(Stoke), Carter (Sunderland), Lawton
(Arsenal), Hagan (Sheffield Un.), Compton
(Arsenal).
After a run of five wins, Wales
have surrendered the lead in the
League Cup qualifying competition.

Services Cup Final Teams

Teams for the Inter-Allied Services
Cup final on Whit-Monday will be
of international strength. They are:
R.A.F.: Bartram (Charlton), Scott and B Jo
Hapgood (Arsenal), Crayston and B Jones
Kirchen (Arsenal), Buckingham, Scott and
Fenton (Middlesbrough), Brown (Tottenham),
chester C.) and O'Donnell, Doherty (Charlton)
Army (from): Swift (Manchester C.)
Bacuzzi (Fulham), Beattie, A (Preston),
Sproston (Manchester C.); Britton (Ever-
ton), Cullis (Wolverhampton), Mercer (Ever-
castle), Goslin (Bolton); Birkett (New-
(Charlton), Hagan (Sheffield U.), Welsh
ton, D (Arsenal) and Sabin (Cardiff).

34

Many professional footballers volunteered for the forces in 1939. Forty out of forty-two Arsenal players joined up. Some teams lost their grounds - Arsenal had to share White Hart Lane with Tottenham. Plymouth and Dundee United were forced to close down for a time. One curious result of the war was that games between the Forces teams were often like internationals.

Some other sports suffered more than football. There were no County Cricket Championship matches played during the war, and no Wimbledon tennis championships. Amateur sport was hit too. Not only were many young men away from home, but playing fields were sometimes ploughed up. However, there were some who were determined to enjoy their sport whatever the dangers. Richmond Golf Club made up new rules. One was:

A player whose stroke is affected by the simultaneous explosion of a bomb or shell may play another ball from the same place. Penalty one stroke.

Longmate *How We Lived Then*

1. Why would a game between, say, the Army and the R.A.F. be like an international match?
2. Why do you think playing fields were sometimes ploughed up?
3. Why do you think the Government did not stop sport, including football and golf, altogether?

(This would be a good time to do Workguide 8.)

10. Victory

For months the people of southern England had watched. Huge numbers of soldiers and great dumps of supplies and equipment were appearing near the south coast. Everyone knew that something important must be happening, but no one knew exactly what.

Then on the radio and in newspapers, on 6 and 7 June 1944 all was revealed. Read what a newspaper reporter wrote:

Guns are belching flame from more than 600 Allied warships. Thousands of bombers are roaring overhead, and fighters are weaving in and out of the clouds. The invasion of Europe has begun.

We are standing some 8 000 yards [*about 7 000 metres*] off the beaches and from the bridge of this destroyer I can see vast numbers of naval craft. In ten minutes more than 2 000 tons [*tonnes*] of H. E. shells have gone down on the beachhead. It is now exactly 7.25 am and through my glasses I can see the first wave of assault troops touching down on the water's edge and fan up the beach.

Daily Mirror 7 June 1944

1. What do you think the reporter was watching?

This was D-Day — the day the Allied armies

British troops return to France after four years. Part of the assault force landing in Normandy, 6 June 1944. Less than one year later Hitler was dead and Germany had surrendered.

landed in Normandy. American, British and Canadian troops took part, under the command of the American General Eisenhower. Careful plans had been made. Secrecy had been vital. The Germans must not know of the plan. Despite this, there was some fierce fighting, especially where the Americans landed. Yet they held on; the British army, with its powerful ally, had returned to France after four years. The liberation of Europe from Nazi control had begun. ('D-Day' was short for 'Deliverance Day'.)

1. *What had happened four years before D-Day?*
2. *How do you think the British people would greet the news of the Normandy landings?*

The End at Last

Britain had never seen a day like it. It was 8 May 1945. People were celebrating everywhere. In London crowds stood outside Buckingham Palace.

We all walked to Buckingham Palace. As we got in front of it the floodlighting flicked on. It was wonderful. Then the King and Queen and the two Princesses came onto the balcony. We yelled and yelled and yelled and waved and cheered. They waved back to us. It was wonderful.

We went to a huge bonfire in the Park. People had joined hands and were circling round it.

Longmate *How We Lived The*

VE Day celebrations in Leicester Square, London. Notice the number of people in uniform, and compare the expressions of the crowd with those on page 4.

That night there were many bonfires. Glasgow Fire Brigade was called to 70 bonfires that were out of control. A film was interrupted at the Regal in Edinburgh, to play the National Anthem; then the audience stood and cheered.

1. *What do you think was the cause of these celebrations? (The Time-Line inside the back cover will help.)*
2. *Find out who were the King, Queen and two Princesses mentioned.*

This was V E Day. The war against Germany had come to an end, but it was to be another three months before the Second World War actually ended. The Japanese finally surrendered on September 2nd. At last the war was really over. The long, hard work of recovery and rebuilding could begin. It was to be many years, however, before the scars of war disappeared from Britain. Bomb damaged buildings took years to rebuild. Rationing continued until 1953. Above all, there were those who had lost relatives or friends, or who had been crippled by injury. For them the war might never end. But for most people, there was the hope of a new and better Britain.

1. *Some servicemen were away from their families for up to four years. One soldier had last seen his son when he was six months old in 1940. How would father - and son - feel when they met in 1945?*
2. *Why do you think VE Day was celebrated with greater enthusiasm than VJ Day?*

(Now would be a good time to do Workguide 9.)

The original caption to this picture said 'Sergeant Ford of the Rifle Brigade savours a long-awaited moment on a railway platform'.

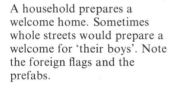

11. Finding Out About the War

The Second World War happened within living memory. This means it is unlike many of the other topics studied in history at school. Most of our history is about things which happened long ago.

One advantage of this is that we can study many 'primary sources', that is information that comes from the time of the war, from those who were in it. There are news-reels and other documentary films, radio recordings, photographs, newspapers, the writings or memories of people who remember, and artefacts [objects], from wartime. Some of the items you might be able to find are illustrated here.

Look also for old photographs, newspapers and magazines. Speak to people you know. Search for interesting things connected with the war. Another way to find out about it is to look for books in your library. Some of the books you may find are listed in the bibliography opposite.

A household prepares a welcome home. Sometimes whole streets would prepare a welcome for 'their boys'. Note the foreign flags and the prefabs.

Bibliography

Books on the 'Home Front'

Bishop, E.   *Their Finest Hour (Purnell's History of World War II, Battle Book No. 2)*   Macdonald 1968.

†Calder, A.   *The People's War 1939-45*   Cape 1969 (Panther 1979)

Caws, B.W. & Watts, R.F.   *The Earthquake Hour. A Scrapbook of the Second World War*   Blackie 1975

Deighton, L.   *The Battle of Britain*   Book Club Associates (and Jonathan Cape) 1980

Divine, D.   *The Nine Days of Dunkirk*   Faber 1959 (White Lion 1976)

Fitzgibbon, C.   *The Blitz*   Macdonald 1970

†Harrison, T.   *Living Through the Blitz*   Penguin 1978

Home Front — News Items from 1939-45   Aberdeen College of Education 1977

Judd, D.   *Posters of World War Two*   Wayland 1972

*Kelsall, F.   *How We Used to Live 1925-45*   Macdonald 1976

†Longmate, N.   *How We Lived Then*   Hutchinson 1971   *The Real Dad's Army*   Hutchinson 1974   *When We Won the War*   Hutchinson 1977

Marwick, A.   *The Home Front. The British and the Second World War*   Thames & Hudson 1976

* Monham, K.   *Growing up in World War II*   Wayland 1979

Mosley, L.   *World War II — The Battle of Britain*   Time-Life Inc 1977

* Reynoldson, F.   *The War at Home*   Heinemann 1980

Sources for Central Scotland   (Vol. 3 — World War Two), Central Region Education Authority 1977

The War Papers   (reprints of wartime newspapers) Peter Way and Cavendish Marshall Partworks Ltd. 1976-7

Memoirs

Allingham, M.   *The Oaken Heart*   (wartime in a country village) Michael Joseph 1941

Hillary, R.   *The Last Enemy*   (a personal account by a Battle of Britain pilot) Macmillan 1942 (Pan 1969)

Panter-Downes, M.   *London War Notes 1939-45*   ed. W. Shawn   Longman 1972

Richardson, M.L.   *London's Burning*   R. Hale 1941

Brief Accounts of the Second World War

* Bayne-Jardine, C.   *World War Two (Modern Times)*   Longman 1968

* Hobley, L.F.   *The Second World War (Topics in Modern History)*   Blackie 1971

* Peacock, R.   *The Second World War (Signposts to History)*   Macmillan 1974

* Reynoldson, F.   *The World at War*   Heinemann 1980

* Snellgrove, L.E.   *World War II (Making the Modern World, Europe)*,   Longman 1970

There were many booklets concerning the work of civil defence and other services, and local experiences of the blitz published during and immediately after the war. For example,   *Front Line 1940-41*   (HMSO 1942) tells the story of Civil Defence.   *Merchantmen at War*   (HMSO 1944) tells of the Merchant Navy.   *Bombers over Merseyside*   (Liverpool Daily Post & Echo 1943) describes the blitz there. They are well illustrated.

Pupils will also find much of interest in the wide variety of larger illustrated works on the war, such as Purnell's   *History of the Second World War.*

Audio Visual Material
Filmstrips and Slides

City Under Fire   The story of the London Blitz (colour with cassette) Wheaton

The Second World War   (in two parts, black and white, *Common Ground* series) Longman

Sound Recording

BBC Scrapbook for 1940   Fontana

The Sounds of All Our Yesterdays   Transatlantic Records

* Specifically for younger pupils
† Specifically for adults

39

Index

Air raids 3-4, 18-24, 32
Anderson shelters 22
ARP - precautions 4-9
  - services 23-24

Barrage balloons 5
Battle of Britain 16-17
'Bevin Boys' 30
Bevin, Ernest 30
Blackout 5-6
'Blitz' the, 18-24 (see also Air raids)
Blitzkrieg 10

Chamberlain, Neville 4, 13
Churchill, Winston 13-14, 17
Cinemas 32-33
Clothing 28-29
Clydebank 20-21
Conscription ('Call-up') 30
Convoys 25
Coventry 19-20

Dancing 33
D-Day 35
Declaration of war 4
Dig for Victory 27
Dunkirk 11-13

Eisenhower, General 35
Entertainment 32-33
Essential work 30

Evacuation 7-9
  towns evacuated 8

Farming 28, 31
Fire-bombs 19
Fire brigades 19, 24
Food 26
Football 33-34
France 10-11, 14, 35

Gas (and masks) 5, 7, 10
Glasgow 9, 20, 37
Goering, Hermann 17
Government restrictions 6, 26, 28, 30

Hitler 14, 17
Home Guard 16

Incendiaries (see Fire-bombs)
Industry 28, 30-31
Invasion of France 10
  Low Countries 10
  Normandy 35
  Poland 4, 10

Land Army 31
Local Defence Volunteers (see Home
  Guard)
London, 5, 9, 16, 18-19, 23-24, 36

Merchant Navy 25
Mining 30

Normandy landings 35

Operation Dynamo 11
Operation Sealion 14, 17

Preparations to meet invasion 15-16

Radio 4, 15, 32
RAF 16-17
Rationing of food 26-27, 37
  clothes 28-29
Royal Navy 11, 25

Shelters (air-raid) 3, 22-23
Sirens 3, 18
Sport 32-34
Submarines 25

Towns evacuated 8
  bombed 20
Tube stations (see Underground)

Underground stations — as shelters
  for industry 30

V1 and V2 rockets 24
VE Day 36-37
VJ Day 37

Wardens (ARP) 23-24
'Welcome Home' 37-38
Women's work 30-31